Slimmericks

Laugh and Lose Weight

by

Richard Davidson

Slimmericks   Richard Davidson

Books by Richard Davidson:
Self-help:
DECISION TIME! Better Decisions for a Better Life
Mysteries:
The Lord's Prayer Mystery Series:
Lead Us Not into Temptation
Give Us this Day Our Daily Bread
Forgive Us Our Trespasses
Thy Will Be Done
Deliver Us from Evil
Imp Mysteries:
Implications
Impulses
Impostor
Impending
Impasse
Historically Based Fiction
Loyalties
Anthology: (Editor)
Overcoming: An Anthology by the Writers of OCWW
Humor: *Slimmericks*

This book is a work of humor. Contents of this book do not constitute medical advice. See your medical professional for advice regarding weight loss and fitness.

Slimmericks, by Richard Davidson
ISBN 978-0-9976381-5-8
Laugh and Lose Weight

Cover Photo by Tamara Bellis on Unsplash

There once was a woman named Mabel

Who pushed herself away from the table.

She lost lots of weight,

And kept feeling great,

But divorced her hefty mate, Abel.

Slimmericks   Richard Davidson

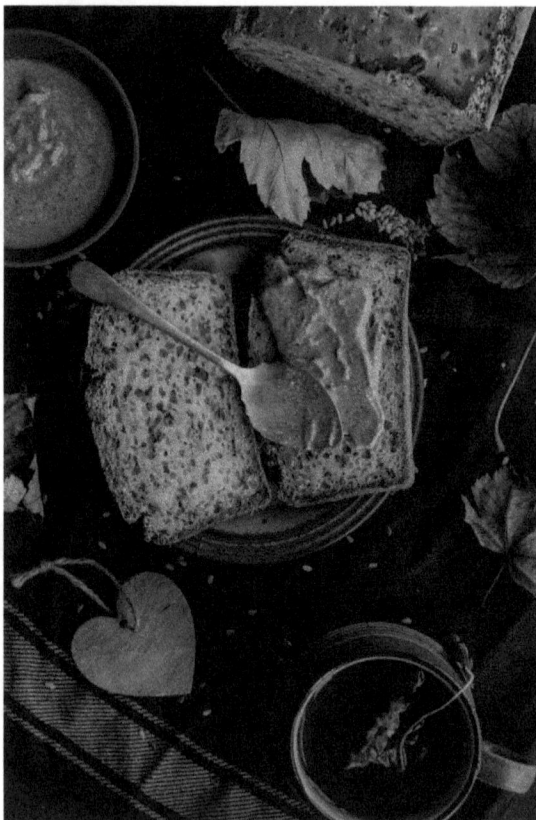

Peanut butter goes well with jelly

And often sits well in your belly.

But don't eat in a rush

Or you'll have to flush

And miss your sheduled show on the telly.

Photo by Thomas Lipke on Unsplash

A beer is a drink of delight,

Especially when consumed at night

While watching a sport

With your favorite cohort

'til you find your belt is too tight.

Slimmericks   Richard Davidson

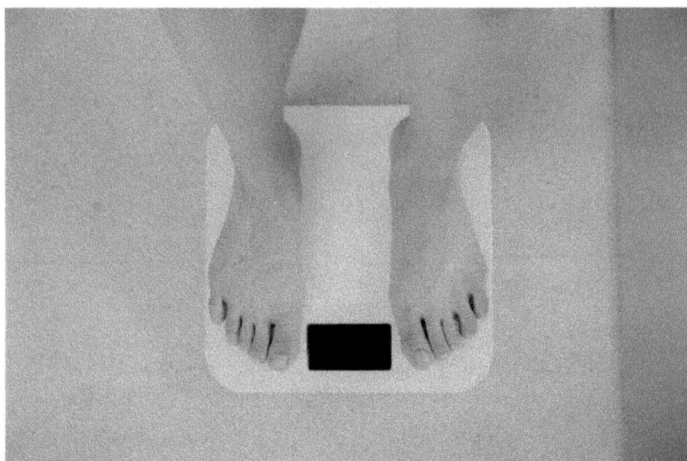

A scale is the devil's torment

Despite all of your good intent.

Ignore what it's reading

And keep right on feeding

Label its dial, "Space for rent."

Photo by Marc Schäfer on Unsplash

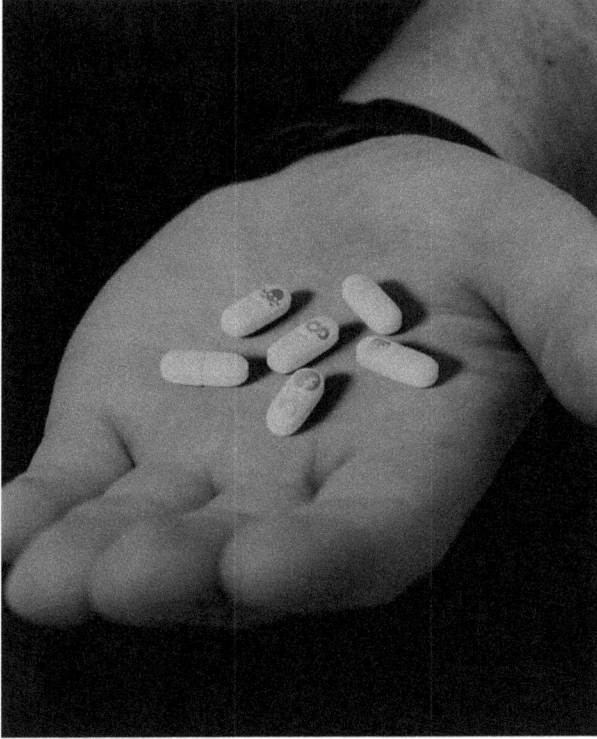

Vitamins we take every day

Even when our doctors say

They don't do a thing

To give you more zing,

But still we buy them and we pay.

Photo by Mathieu Turle on Unsplash

A charming young lady named Brenda

Thought she was amazingly slender.

Ate small with a dash

That left her more cash,

Which was good for she was a big spender.

Slimmericks   Richard Davidson

A sporty young man named Barry

Ate all the food he could carry.

He started to bloat

While out on his boat

To the head he must go without tarry.

Photo by Katarina Šikuljak on Unsplash

The exercise bug must have bit me.

I feel guilty whenever I sit me.

I balance and stretch

'til I want to retch,

But my very old trousers still fit me.

Slimmericks   Richard Davidson

A very young child named Dakota

Would not drink any sweet soda.

She drank water instead

Sometimes colored it red.

She was wise, just like friend Yoda.

Slimmericks   Richard Davidson

A man who sat out on a beach

Ate snack foods and even a peach.

He lay in the sun

'til digestion was done,

His sunburn, when touched, made him screech.

Slimmericks   Richard Davidson

A man read about a new diet,

But when he decided to try it

He found it cost more

Than food from the store,

He saved cash and didn't go buy it.

Slimmericks   Richard Davidson

If you eat more and exercise less

You'll find yourself in a mess.

Forget diet talk.

Just go out for a walk,

And once more you'll fit in that dress.

Slimmericks   Richard Davidson

A menu of just beans and rice

Is bound to help you out twice.

You'll sit on the pot;

You'll lose weight a lot;

And all for a very low price.

Slimmericks   Richard Davidson

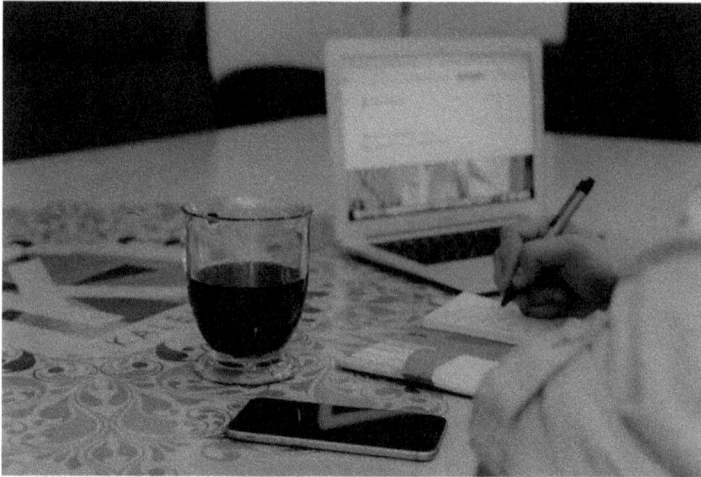

Don't listen to all of the ads

About untried new diet fads.

Get back on the bike

Eat bits that you like

Log your eating on old paper pads.

Slimmericks   Richard Davidson

Your snacks are the devil's delight.

He wants you to eat them all night.

Just close up that box

And be a smart fox

That keeps moving and makes muscles tight.

Slimmericks   Richard Davidson

If snacking's a thing you must do

You'll have to try plan number two.

Just don't eat your dinner

And you'll be a winner,

But try to snack vegetables too.

Photo by Yasuo Takeuchi on Unsplash

If you drink water all day

You'll feel full at work or at play.

You'll be at your best

And won't need a rest

Unless in the bathroom you stay.

Photo by Jade Wulfraat on Unsplash

Don't fret about each thing you eat.

You deserve an occasional treat.

If a snack's not a habit,

It's OK to grab it,

But don't make it overly sweet.

Photo by Toa Heftiba on Unsplash

That apple pie looks oh so good.

Will I eat it or pass as I should?

I'll take just one bite

And lock it up tight

So I'll have no choice but to be good.

Slimmericks   Richard Davidson

It's no fun to drink coffee alone.

It would go oh so well with a scone.

But I'll do my best

To withstand the test

And chew on Rover's dog bone.

They want you to drink lots of water.

They always say that you oughta.

They say coffee don't count,

Not in any amount.

I say "they" oughta be shota.

Slimmericks   Richard Davidson

Photo by Nhia Moua on Unsplash

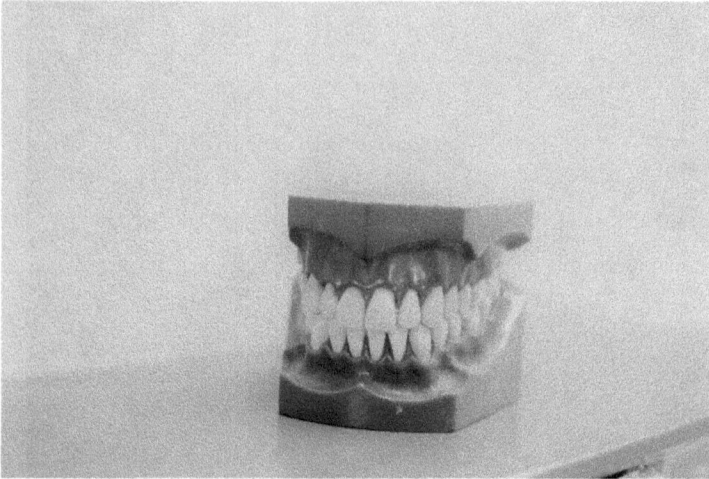

If you chew every bite many times

You'll reduce many solids to slimes.

But you will lose weight;

Your teeth you will grate.

To the dentist you'll give many dimes.

Photo by Maëliss Demaison on Unsplash

One thousand calories per day

Will get you well on your way

That's what the doc said

As I lay on the bed

Staring at yogurt on my tray.

Photo by Matheus Ferrero on Unsplash

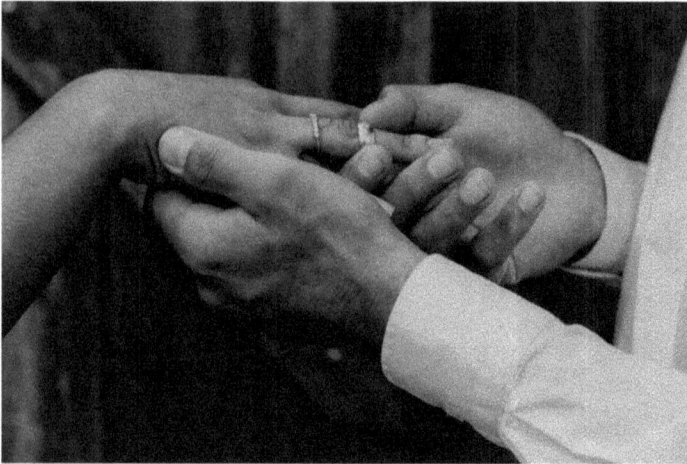

When you first hear that word "obese"

You'll wish nasty comments would cease.

But you'll understand

Why a friend holds your hand

So you can't eat all that you please.

Slimmericks   Richard Davidson

If you want to lose lots of weight

Eat only foods that you hate.

You'll eat very few

For a much slimmer you

And you'll end up feeling just great.

Slimmericks   Richard Davidson

For a body that you'll find adoring

Eat the same foods 'til they're boring.

Repeat and repeat

Makes you not want to eat.

You'll go lie on the couch and start snoring.

Photo by Lizzie on Unsplash

An uncomfortable seat at your table

Ejects you as soon as you're able.

You won't eat too much

With a bottom sore to touch

And your weight will decrease or be stable

Slimmericks   Richard Davidson

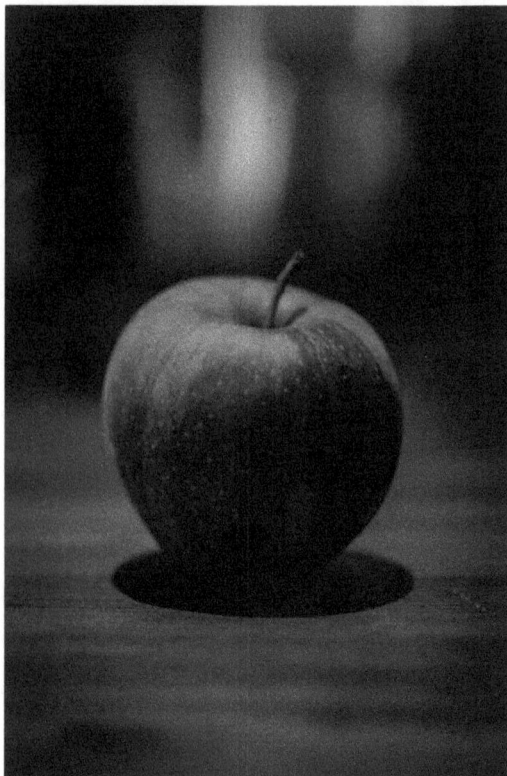

Apples keep the old doctor away

And they also help you to play.

With few calories

They're so bound to please

And they let you stay active all day.

Slimmericks   Richard Davidson

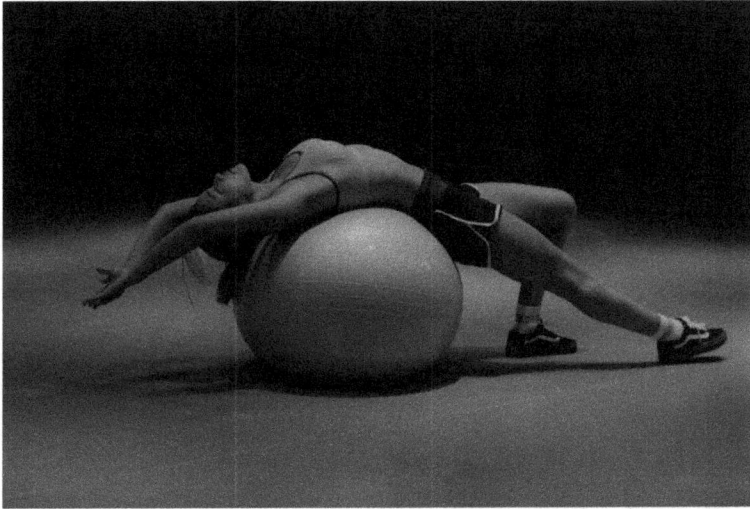

An exercise routine in your home

Gives you extra freedom to roam.

No workout classes

For both lads and lasses

You'll have time to write out a poem.

Slimmericks   Richard Davidson

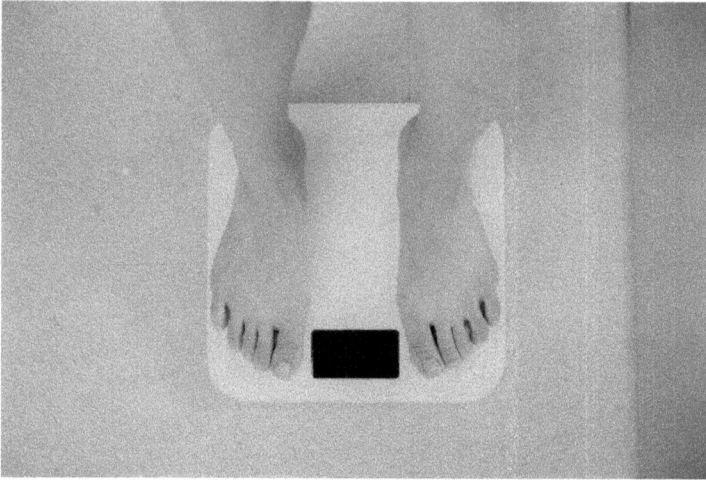

All meals shouldn't be the same size

If you want to take weight off those thighs.

Eat more morns and noons,

Later, just a few spoons.

Morning scale shows a pleasant surprise.

Slimmericks   Richard Davidson

Write what you eat in a book.

You'll be shocked when you give it a look.

So many quick snacks

It's time to relax

Stealing nibbles makes you a food crook.

Slimmericks   Richard Davidson

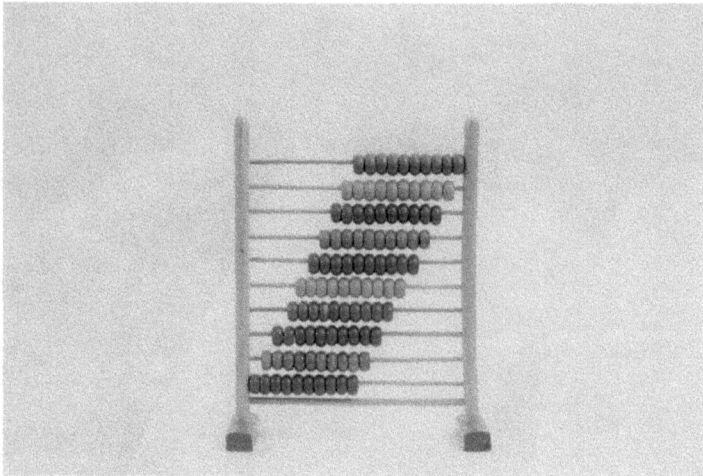

A calorie counter named Stu

Used an abacus to make his counts true.

He slid many beads

At each one of his feeds

But his total passed his limit times two.

Slimmericks   Richard Davidson

Have you noticed how food that's gourmet

At the restaurant is smaller each day

It looks so top-rate

In the middle of your plate

And your wallet loses weight when you pay.

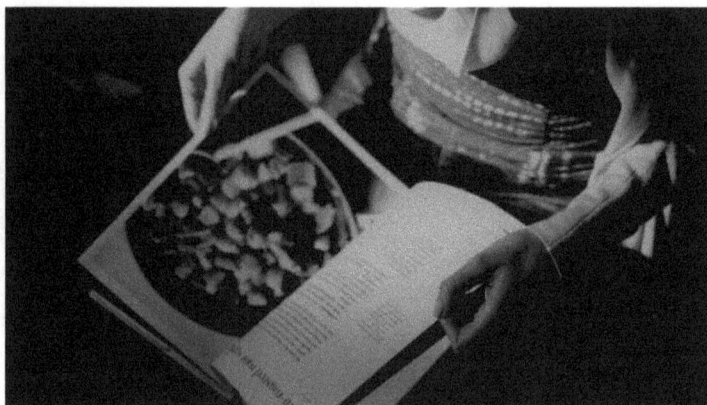

I think I'll write a cookbook

That deserves every dieter's look.

The pages will be blank,

For, my dear, let's be frank.

Calorie-free is water from a brook.

Photo by Jenna Anderson on Unsplash

On a beach a pretty girl walks past,

The man sucks his belly in fast.

If he could repeat

That same thing on the street

He'd shape up and make life a blast.

Slimmericks   Richard Davidson

If food had big calorie labels

We'd keep most of it off of our tables.

Five calorie pickles would pass

As would water in our glass

Don't believe that; it's one of our fables.

Photo by i yunmai on Unsplash

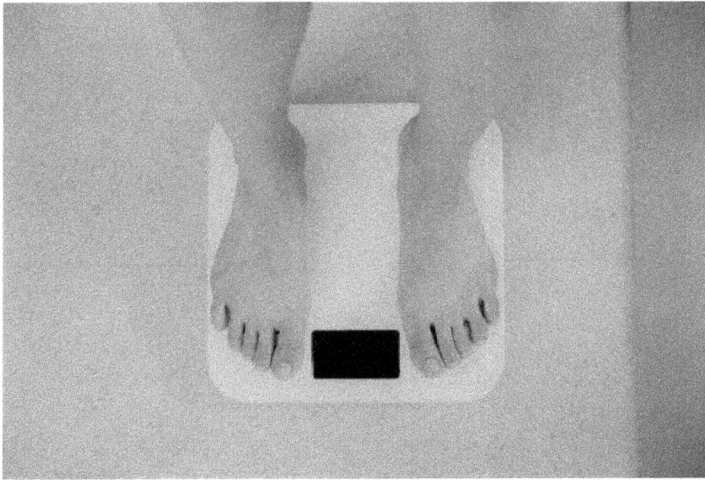

If you have put on too much weight

Buy a new scale to see how you rate.

But if, truth be told

New reads higher than old,

Return it right after you've ate.

Slimmericks   Richard Davidson

And when all is said and is done,

Losing weight isn't much fun.

Trade a meal for a nap

No calories; it's a snap.

Rip Van Winkle could sleep off a ton.

Photo by Clem Onojeghuo on Unsplash

Those long sweaty sessions at the gym

Won't definitely make you get slim.

They'll build up your bod,

Make you gasp, "Oh, my God,"

But your hopes of great weight loss are dim.

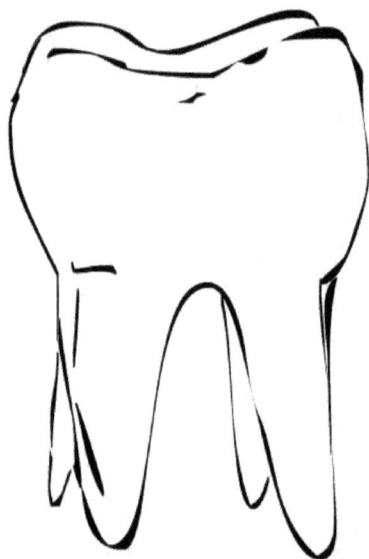

A certain young woman named Ruth

Understood the weight losing truth.

Calories reduced plus calories burned

Is 3500 per one pound loss earned

Or the dentist pulls your one pound tooth.

Slimmericks   Richard Davidson

A beautiful woman named Mary

Lost weight in a way quite contrary.

She wore fishnet clothes

And peek-a-boo hose

To the rest of us she looked quite scary.

Slimmericks   Richard Davidson

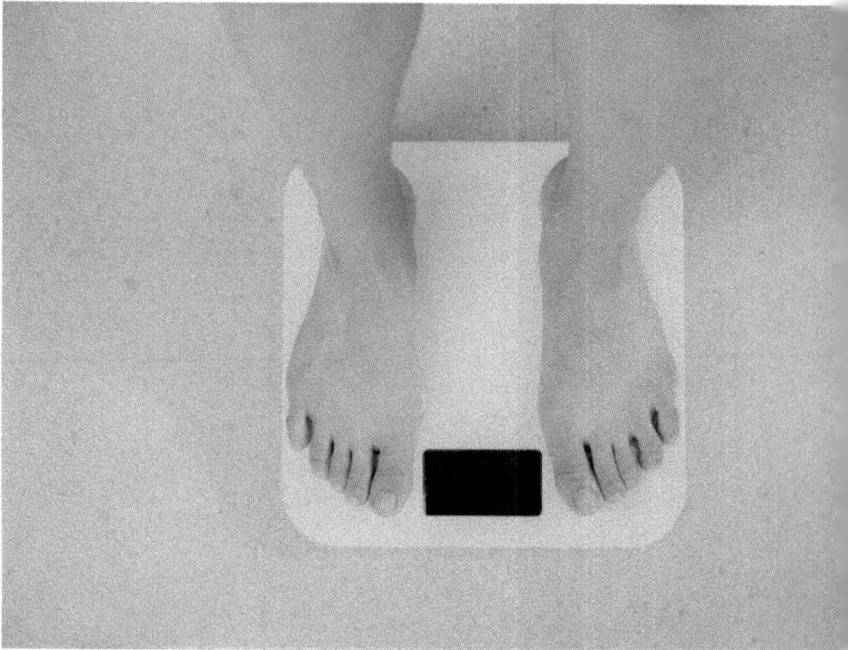

Early each morning without fail

Visit your trusty bathroom scale.

The number by your feet

Tells you how much you can eat

If your health wish is to prevail.

Slimmericks   Richard Davidson

When dining out on food Chinese,

There's a slim tip that's bound to please.

If all share their dish

And donate some fish

You'll enjoy, and have shared lower fees.

Slimmericks   Richard Davidson

When to a restaurant you go,

Make a doggy bag part of the show.

Take leftovers away

For extra meals without pay,

And your calorie count will be low.

Slimmericks   Richard Davidson

My closet is full of thin clothes

Due to optimism I suppose

I can't lose much weight

Willpower's second rate,

Young memories tie me to those.

45

Slimmericks   Richard Davidson

Then there's the matter of my belt.

A beauty from when I was svelte.

I so deeply regret

Tongue and buckle haven't met

Ever since my round tummy I felt.

Photo by Maëliss Demaison on Unsplash

So now I must face facts at last.

My trim body's a thing of the past.

I'll try to get thin,

Though I'll never win,

And I'll walk by the mirror very fast.

Acknowledgments

The source of the tooth illustration is Public Domain Clip Art (www.pdclipart.org).

Photographs are individually credited above the illustrations. They come from Unsplash: Photos for everyone (https://unsplash.com).